THE ORANGE
AND OTHER POEMS

WENDY COPE

THE ORANGE
and other poems

faber

First published in 2023
by Faber & Faber Ltd
The Bindery, 51 Hatton Garden
London EC1N 8HN

Typeset by Typo•glyphix, Burton-on-Trent DE14 3HE
Printed and bound in Great Britain by TJ Books Limited

A CIP record for this book
is available from the British Library

ISBN 978-0-571-38951-3

4 6 8 10 9 7 5

Contents

THE ORANGE
AND OTHER POEMS

Valentine

My heart has made its mind up
And I'm afraid it's you.
Whatever you've got lined up,
My heart has made its mind up
And if you can't be signed up
This year, next year will do.
My heart has made its mind up
And I'm afraid it's you

The Orange

At lunchtime I bought a huge orange –
The size of it made us all laugh.
I peeled it and shared it with Robert and Dave –
They got quarters and I had a half.

And that orange, it made me so happy,
As ordinary things often do
Just lately. The shopping. A walk in the park.
This is peace and contentment. It's new.

The rest of the day was quite easy.
I did all the jobs on my list
And enjoyed them and had some time over.
I love you. I'm glad I exist.

Flowers

Some men never think of it.
You did. You'd come along
And say you'd nearly brought me flowers
But something had gone wrong.

The shop was closed. Or you had doubts –
The sort that minds like ours
Dream up incessantly. You thought
I might not want your flowers.

It made me smile and hug you then.
Now I can only smile.
But, look, the flowers you nearly brought
Have lasted all this while.

At 3 a.m.

the room contains no sound
except the ticking of the clock
which has begun to panic
like an insect, trapped
in an enormous box.

Books lie open on the carpet.

Somewhere else
you're sleeping
and beside you there's a woman
who is crying quietly
so you won't wake.

Loss

The day he moved out was terrible –
That evening she went through hell.
His absence wasn't a problem
But the corkscrew had gone as well.

Two Cures for Love

1. Don't see him. Don't phone or write a letter.
2. The easy way: get to know him better.

Defining the Problem

I can't forgive you. Even if I could,
You wouldn't pardon me for seeing through you.
And yet I cannot cure myself of love
For what I thought you were before I knew you.

I Worry

I worry about you –
So long since we spoke.
Love, are you downhearted,
Dispirited, broke?

I worry about you.
I can't sleep at night.
Are you sad? Are you lonely?
Or are you all right?

They say that men suffer,
As badly, as long.
I worry, I worry,
In case they are wrong.

Faint Praise

Size isn't everything. It's what you do
That matters, darling, and you do quite well
In some respects. Credit where credit's due –
You work, you're literate, you rarely smell.
Small men can be aggressive, people say,
But you are often genial and kind,
As long as you can have things all your way
And I comply, and do not speak my mind.
You look all right. I've never been disgusted
By paunchiness. Who wants some skinny youth?
My friends have warned me that you can't be trusted
But I protest I've heard you tell the truth.
Nobody's perfect. Now and then, my pet,
You're almost human. You could make it yet.

Some More Light Verse

You have to try. You see a shrink.
You learn a lot. You read. You think.
You struggle to improve your looks.
You meet some men. You write some books.
You eat good food. You give up junk.
You do not smoke. You don't get drunk.
You take up yoga, walk and swim.
And nothing works. The outlook's grim.
You don't know what to do. You cry.
You're running out of things to try.

You blow your nose. You see the shrink.
You walk. You give up food and drink.
You fall in love. You make a plan.
You struggle to improve your man.
And nothing works. The outlook's grim.
You go to yoga, cry, and swim.
You eat and drink. You give up looks.
You struggle to improve your books.
You cannot see the point. You sigh.
You do not smoke. You have to try.

After the Lunch

On Waterloo Bridge, where we said our goodbyes,
The weather conditions bring tears to my eyes.
I wipe them away with a black woolly glove
And try not to notice I've fallen in love.

On Waterloo Bridge I am trying to think:
This is nothing. You're high on the charm and the drink.
But the juke-box inside me is playing a song
That says something different. And when was it wrong?

On Waterloo Bridge with the wind in my hair
I am tempted to skip. *You're a fool.* I don't care.
The head does its best but the heart is the boss –
I admit it before I am halfway across.

Favourite

When they ask me, 'Who's your favourite poet?'
I'd better not mention you,
Though you certainly are my favourite poet
And I like your poems too.

Magnetic

i spell it out on this fridge door
you are so wonderful
i even like th   way you snor

Nine-line Triolet

Here's a fine mess we got ourselves into,
My angel, my darling, true love of my heart
Etcetera. Must stop it but I can't begin to.
Here's a fine mess we got ourselves into –
Both in a spin with nowhere to spin to,
Bound by the old rules in life and in art.
Here's a fine mess we got ourselves into,
(I'll curse every rule in the book as we part)
My angel, my darling, true love of my heart.

Seeing You

Seeing you will make me sad.
I want to do it anyway.
We can't relive the times we had –
Seeing you will make me sad.
Perhaps it's wrong. Perhaps it's mad.
But we will both be dead one day.
Seeing you will make me sad.
I have to do it anyway.

Dutch Portraits

To find myself in tears is a surprise –
Paintings don't often get to me like this:
These faces with their vulnerable eyes
And lips so soft that they invite a kiss;
The long-haired husband, gazing at his bride
With evident desire, his hand around
Her wrist, six years before she died –
Both so alive and so long underground.
And here's a husband who resembles you
When you were plump and bearded. It's too much.
He looks so happy and his wife does too,
Still smiling, now they can no longer touch.
Someone will read our story, by and by.
Perhaps they'll feel like this. Perhaps they'll cry.

The Uncertainty of the Poet

'The Tate Gallery yesterday announced that it had
paid £1 million for a Giorgio de Chirico masterpiece,
The Uncertainty of the Poet. It depicts a torso and
a bunch of bananas.' – *Guardian*, 2 April 1985

I am a poet.
I am very fond of bananas.

I am bananas.
I am very fond of a poet.

I am a poet of bananas.
I am very fond,

A fond poet of 'I am, I am' –
Very bananas,

Fond of 'Am I bananas,
Am I?' – a very poet.

Bananas of a poet!
Am I fond? Am I very?

Poet bananas! I am.
I am fond of a 'very'.

I am of very fond bananas.
Am I a poet?

Haiku

A perfect white wine
is sharp, sweet and cold as this:
birdsong in winter.

By the River

The day is so still
you can almost hear the heat.
You can almost hear
that royal blue dragonfly
landing on the old white boat.

Names

She was Eliza for a few weeks
When she was a baby –
Eliza Lily. Soon it changed to Lil.

Later she was Miss Steward in the baker's shop
And then 'my love', 'my darling', Mother.

Widowed at thirty, she went back to work
As Mrs Hand. Her daughter grew up,
Married and gave birth.

Now she was Nanna. 'Everybody
Calls me Nanna,' she would say to visitors.
And so they did – friends, tradesmen, the doctor.

In the geriatric ward
They used the patients' Christian names.
'Lil,' we said, 'or Nanna,'
But it wasn't in her file
And for those last bewildered weeks
She was Eliza once again.

Tich Miller

Tich Miller wore glasses
with elastoplast-pink frames
and had one foot three sizes larger than the other.

When they picked teams for outdoor games
she and I were always the last two
left standing by the wire-mesh fence.

We avoided one another's eyes,
stooping, perhaps, to re-tie a shoelace,
or affecting interest in the flight

of some fortunate bird, and pretended
not to hear the urgent conference:
'Have Tubby!' 'No, no, have Tich!'

Usually they chose me, the lesser dud,
and she lolloped, unselected,
to the back of the other team.

At eleven we went to different schools.
In time I learned to get my own back,
sneering at hockey-players who couldn't spell.

Tich died when she was twelve.

Absent Friends

'The ones we remember are those linked
with things we do all the time'
– Katharine Whitehorn

Roz

My school friend Roz, who died twenty years ago,
pulled her cardigan down at the back
every time she stood up and crossed a room.

Whenever I glance in a mirror
and see that my cardigan has ridden up
I remember Roz.

She was my rival in English.
The teachers were so impressed
by her passion for Tolkien
that I didn't read *The Lord of the Rings*
until I was fifty-five.

Little Donkey

The children's favourite. We had
to sing it in the Christmas concert
every year, plodding along
with me at the piano, and a child
going clip-clop with coconut shells
or woodblock: a coveted job.

It wasn't my favourite.
After I left teaching
I forgot about it
for more than ten years

until one day, near Christmas,
in a busy high street
a Salvation Army band
began to play it. I stood still

with tears in my eyes.
Little Donkey. All those children
who loved it so much.
All those hands in the air
begging to be chosen
to make the sound of his hooves.

A Christmas Poem

At Christmas little children sing and merry bells jingle,
The cold winter air makes our hands and faces tingle
And happy families go to church and cheerily they
    mingle
And the whole business is unbelievably dreadful, if
    you're single.

Men Talking

Anecdotes and jokes,
On and on and on.
If you're with several blokes,
It's anecdotes and jokes.

If you were to die
Of boredom, there and then,
They'd notice, by and by,
If you were to die.

But it could take a while.
They're having so much fun.
You neither speak nor smile.
It could take a while.

Song

My love got in the car
And sat on my banana,
My unobserved banana
And my organic crisps.

We spoke of life and love,
His rump on my banana,
My hidden, soft banana
And my forgotten crisps.

He kissed me more than once
As he sat on that banana,
That newly-squashed banana
And those endangered crisps.

We looked up at the stars –
Beneath him, my banana,
My saved-from-lunch banana
And my delicious crisps.

At last I dropped him off
And noticed the banana –
Alas, a ruined banana
And sadly damaged crisps.

You'd think he would have felt
A fairly large banana
And, if not the banana,
The lumpy bag of crisps.

But he's the kind of man
Who'll sit on a banana
For hours. Watch your banana
And guard your bag of crisps.

He waved goodbye and smiled,
Benign as a banana.
'I love you, daft banana,'
Said I, and ate the crisps.

Being Boring

'May you live in interesting times.' – Chinese curse

If you ask me 'What's new?', I have nothing to say
Except that the garden is growing.
I had a slight cold but it's better today.
I'm content with the way things are going.
Yes, he is the same as he usually is,
Still eating and sleeping and snoring.
I get on with my work. He gets on with his.
I know this is all very boring.

There was drama enough in my turbulent past:
Tears and passion – I've used up a tankful.
No news is good news, and long may it last.
If nothing much happens, I'm thankful.
A happier cabbage you never did see,
My vegetable spirits are soaring.
If you're after excitement, steer well clear of me.
I want to go on being boring.

I don't go to parties. Well, what are they for,
If you don't need to find a new lover?
You drink and you listen and drink a bit more
And you take the next day to recover.
Someone to stay home with was all my desire
And, now that I've found a safe mooring,
 I've just one ambition in life: I aspire
To go on and on being boring.

He Tells Her
(for Ruth B.)

He tells her that the Earth is flat –
He knows the facts, and that is that.
In altercations fierce and long
She tries her best to prove him wrong.
But he has learned to argue well.
He calls her arguments unsound
And often asks her not to yell.
She cannot win. He stands his ground.

The planet goes on being round.

A Vow

I cannot promise never to be angry;
I cannot promise always to be kind.
You know what you are taking on, my darling –
It's only at the start that love is blind.

And yet I'm still the one you want to be with
And you're the one for me – of that I'm sure.
You are my closest friend, my favourite person,
The lover and the home I've waited for.

I cannot promise that I will deserve you
From this day on. I hope to pass that test.
I love you and I want to make you happy.
I promise I will do my very best.

Evidence

'A great deal of anecdotal evidence suggests
that we respond positively to birdsong.'
– scientific researcher, *Daily Telegraph*, 8 February 2012

Centuries of English verse
Suggest the selfsame thing:
A negative response is rare
When birds are heard to sing.

What's the use of poetry?
You ask. Well, here's a start:
It's anecdotal evidence
About the human heart.

Leaving
(for Dick and Afkham)

Next summer? The summer after?
With luck we've a few more years
Of sunshine and drinking and laughter
And airports and goodbyes and tears.

Acknowledgements

Thanks to Sophie Clarke and Imogen Whiteley, both of whom have taken a keen interest in this project. And special thanks to editor Jane Feaver for being so easy and delightful to work with.